LIFE OF PI

YANN MARTEL

LEVEL 3

SCHOLASTIC

Adapted by: Jane Rollason

Publisher: Jacquie Bloese

Editor: Fiona Davis

Designer: Annette Peppis

Illustration: Rachel Morris

Picture research: Emma Bree

Photo credits:
Cover & pages 4, 5, 27, 54, 57: Courtesy of Twentieth Century Fox Film Corporation.
Page 9: Biosphoto/Superstock.
Page 16: risamay/iStockphoto.
Pages 18 & 19: irabell/iStockphoto.
Page 34 & 35: malerapaso/iStockphoto.
Page 38: Biosphoto/Superstock.
Page 42: Ramberg/iStockphoto.
Pages 58 & 59: J. Morgan/Alamy; N. Nanu, H. Ammar/AFP/ Getty Images; Belomlinsky, azat1976, imacon/iStockphoto.

Published by Scholastic Ltd. 2014

Mary Glasgow Magazines (Scholastic Ltd.)
Euston House
24 Eversholt Street
London NW1 1DB

Printed in Malaysia

Reprinted in 2015, 2016, 2017 and 2018

CONTENTS

	PAGE
Life of Pi	**4–57**
People and places	**4–5**
Chapter 1: Writer's note	**6**
Part One: Pondicherry Chapters 2–11	**8**
Part Two: The Pacific Ocean Chapters 12–42	**17**
Part Three: Hospital, Tomatlán, Mexico Chapters 43–49	**50**
Chapter 50: Writer's note	**56**
Fact File: Three religions	**58–59**
Self-Study Activities	**60–63**
New Words	**64**

PI PATEL

Pi Patel is a young boy from Pondicherry in the south of India. Pi is very interested in religion and he loves animals.

THE PATEL FAMILY

Pi lives with his mother and father and older brother, Ravi. They have a zoo. The star animals are their Bengal tigers.

THE STORY

When Pi is sixteen, the family sail for Canada on a ship called the *Tsimtsum*. This is the start of Pi's amazing adventure. Many years later, Pi meets a Canadian writer. The writer helps Pi tell his story.

THE PACIFIC OCEAN

This is the world's largest ocean.

LIFE OF PI

CHAPTER 1

WRITER'S NOTE

I am a writer from Canada. I went to India to write a story. I wrote for many months, but in the end the story did not work. Before I went back home, I decided to explore the south of India. I arrived in Pondicherry, on the south-east coast.

I was at the Indian Coffee House, on Nehru Street, when an old man started talking to me. I told him I was a writer.

"I know a story that will make you believe in God," he said.

I ordered two more coffees. "Where does this story take place?" I asked.

"It starts right here in Pondicherry – at the zoo. It ends in your country. But you must talk to Pi Patel," he said. "It's his story."

"Where can I find Mr Patel?" I asked.

"In Canada."

I went home to Canada. I searched through nine pages of Patels in the phone book, and then I found him – Mr Pi Patel. He agreed to meet me. We met often as he told me his story.

Pi Patel lives in Toronto. He studied zoology and religion at university. His hair is a bit grey now, although he is only forty. He cooks wonderful meals for me in his kitchen. He has enough food in the cupboards to last his whole life.*

Pi's house is a temple inside. In fact, it is many temples. Ganesha, the Hindu God with an elephant head, is in the hall. The Virgin Mary, mother of Jesus Christ, is in the living room. On a table in the office is a book covered by a cloth. The book is the Qur'an, the holy book of Islam.

Pi is married. He and his wife have a son, a daughter, a dog and a cat. So this story has a happy ending.

Sometimes Pi gets upset when he's telling me his story. After all these years, he still thinks about Richard Parker every day.

This is Pi Patel's story.

* *Zoology* is the scientific study of animals.

PART ONE
PONDICHERRY

CHAPTER 2

Before my father moved to Pondicherry, he owned a hotel in Madras. He had always loved animals, however, and in Pondicherry, he decided to open a zoo. Running a zoo is not easy for a hotelkeeper. The 'guests' never leave their rooms and they receive visitors all day long. There is a lot of cleaning to do because they don't use bathrooms. My father loved the Pondicherry Zoo, but he worried about it too.

I loved growing up in a zoo. The lions woke me at six every morning, roaring loudly. As I ran for the school bus, a sleepy orang-utan waved to me. After school, the elephant searched my pockets for fruit.

People often think animals in the wild are 'happy' because they are 'free'. They imagine a lion. It watches an African sunset, sitting proudly with its family under a beautiful tree. Then bad men catch it and put it in a small cage in a zoo. It sits in its new prison and thinks sadly about its old life.

This is not the way it is.

Animals in the wild never have enough food. They must fight every day to keep their home and they get sick. Are they free?

In the wild, an animal has its own territory where it can find food and water, and avoid danger. A zoo cage is just another territory. Food appears every day, there is always water and there is no need to go hunting. The animal does not feel like a prisoner. It feels like a landowner.

But I know many people think zoos are a bad thing. Close down all the zoos if you want to. Anyway, Pondicherry Zoo no longer exists.

CHAPTER 3

My favourite teacher when I was young was Mr Satish Kumar, my science teacher. One day I saw him at the zoo. He was watching the Indian rhinos. At first, we had only one rhino called Peak. He was lonely and he stopped eating. While my father searched for a second rhino, he put some goats in with Peak for company. It worked brilliantly. Peak loved the goats, and they loved him. When the second rhino arrived, she learnt to love the goats too. The goats watched the rhinos in their pool. The rhinos guarded the goats while they ate. These living arrangements were very popular with the visitors.

Mr Kumar saw me and smiled. 'Hello, Pi!' he said.

'Hello, Mr Kumar. It's good of you to come to the zoo,' I said.

'The zoo is my temple,' he said. 'If our politicians were like these goats and rhinos, we'd have fewer problems in our country.'

'Religion will save us,' I said. Religion was always close to my heart, as you will see.

'Religion is darkness, Pi,' said Mr Kumar. 'Why believe in something that you cannot see, hear or touch?'

I had never heard such words.

'When I was your age, Pi, I had polio – a terrible illness – and I spent all my time in bed,' continued Mr Kumar. 'I asked every day, "Where is God?" God never came. Medicine saved me. When we die, it's the end.'

I said nothing.

Mr Kumar was an atheist – he believed that there was no God, only science. Science was his religion. Mr Kumar was the reason I studied zoology at the University of Toronto.

CHAPTER 4

One Sunday morning, before the zoo opened, Father took me and Ravi into the big cat house. Mother came too. Father looked at us with a very serious face.

'I have an important lesson for you boys today,' he said.

'Is this really necessary?' said Mother. She looked unhappy.

'Yes, it is,' said Father. 'It may save their lives.'

Our Bengal tiger, Mahisha, was in his cage. He roared and the whole building seemed to shake.

'Ravi, Pi, I'm going to show you how dangerous tigers are,' Father said. 'You must never try to touch a tiger or even get close to one. They are not your friends.'

Babu, the keeper, came in with a live goat. Mahisha growled. Babu put the frightened little goat into a small cage next to Mahisha's cage. There was a door between them. Babu pulled open the door. The poor goat disappeared in a few seconds.

Mother, Ravi and I refused to speak to Father for a week. After that, whenever Ravi was angry with me, he always said, 'Wait until we're alone. You're the next goat!'

CHAPTER 5

When I was a baby, my aunt took me to a Hindu temple. I remember the smell, the beautiful colours and a feeling of mystery. Religion entered my body on that day.

I am a Hindu. The world makes sense to me through Hindu eyes. Hindus believe that God is in everything.

CHAPTER 6

I was fourteen when I met Jesus Christ. We were on holiday in Kerala, high in the cool hills. One afternoon I went into the Christian church, but I felt afraid. I had not heard good things about Christianity. I knew the Christian God was an angry god. The first thing I saw was a painting of a man covered in blood. So the things I had heard were true!

But then I met the priest. His name was Father Martin. He told me the Christian story. What a strange story! Humans are always fighting. So God says to his son, 'We can stop humans fighting if I allow them to kill *you*.'

Why did God let his son die?

'Love,' said Father Martin.

Why do people follow this son? He's not so special – he's just a man. Yes, he can stop a storm and walk on water. But any Hindu god can do a hundred times better than that.

'Love,' said Father Martin.

The more I learnt about Jesus Christ, the more I liked him. On the last day of our holiday, I ran to the church.

'Father Martin,' I said, 'I would like to be a Christian, please.'

'You already are, Pi – in your heart,' he said. 'Here in Kerala, you met Christ.'

CHAPTER 7

Islam followed right behind. I was exploring the Muslim area of Pondicherry. Next to the Great Mosque on Mullah Street, there was a line of poor buildings. One was a small shop selling flatbread. I picked a flatbread up. It felt hard.

'Would you like to taste one?' said a voice.

I jumped in the air and the bread fell out of my hands. A man was sitting on the ground, hidden by the sunlight.

'I'm so sorry, sir. I didn't see you!' I said.

'Don't worry,' he said. 'The birds will eat it. Have another one.'

I ate it very slowly. The man invited me into his house, which had two rooms. He made bread in the larger room. The other room was his bedroom. As he was showing me the hot stones for cooking the bread, we heard the imam* calling from the mosque. It was time to pray.

'Excuse me,' he said. Right there, he prayed with his eyes closed. I felt uncomfortable. He stood, fell to his knees, sat up, fell forwards again and stood. He repeated the whole thing four times, all the time speaking in Arabic. Finally, he stood silently for a few moments. Then he opened his eyes and smiled.

'What was I saying?' he asked.

I visited him again. He told me Islam is a beautiful religion – a religion of loving your brothers. We went to the mosque. We listened to the imam until the time came to pray. When we brought our heads to the ground, I felt the love of God.

The breadmaker's religion was personal and loving. 'If you take two steps towards God,' he told me, 'God runs to you!'

* An *imam* is an Islamic priest.

CHAPTER 8

One Sunday afternoon, I was walking with my parents in the park. At the very same moment, I saw the Christian priest, the Hindu pandit* and the Muslim imam. Each was on a different path coming towards us. At a point where the four paths met, they all said 'hello' to me.

My parents were surprised. They didn't know I was a Hindu, a Christian and a Muslim. My family were not religious. Father was part of the New India, which was rich and modern. Mother was bored by religion. Ravi's religion was cricket.

'Your son is a good Christian boy,' said the priest.

'You've made a mistake,' said the imam. 'He's a good Muslim boy.'

'You're both wrong,' said the pandit. 'He comes to the Hindu temple all the time.'

The three men all turned to look at me. Before I could speak, each began to explain that his religion was better than the others.

'Gentlemen, please!' said Father. 'We may follow any religion we like in this country.'

'Mr Patel,' said the pandit. 'We are all happy that Pi is so interested in God. But he can't be a Hindu, a Christian and a Muslim. He must choose.'

Everyone looked at me again.

'Pi,' said Mother, 'What do you think?'

'I just want to love God,' I said.

Mother smiled. The three men had no answer. They left us. They were smiling, but they were not happy.

'Ice-cream anyone?' Father asked.

* A *pandit* is a Hindu priest.

CHAPTER 9

In the middle of the 1970s, there was trouble in India. Political trouble is not good for zoos. People cannot enjoy the animals if they are worried about their jobs. We were not a rich family. We were a poor family that owned a lot of animals.

Father wanted to build a future for his sons. As things got worse in India, Father and Mother made a decision.

'We're moving to Canada,' they told Ravi and me.

Canada! It was icy cold in Canada. They didn't play cricket in Canada. And it was as far away as the moon.

CHAPTER 10

We closed the zoo. We sold many of the animals to zoos in North America, and we agreed to travel with them across the ocean. Moving a zoo is like moving a city, and it took more than a year to arrange all the papers for the animals. During that time, Ravi and I came to like the idea of Canada. Finally, we were ready to go.

CHAPTER 11

We left Madras on June the 21st, 1977, on the Japanese ship, *Tsimtsum*. Mother looked sad as we left India. But Father, Ravi and I were in a hurry to get to Canada.

The animals were safe in their cages. Father had given them sleeping pills before the ship left. I was outside on deck, waving wildly to India. I was very excited.

Things didn't happen in the way we expected, but what can you do? You must take life as it comes, and make the best of it.

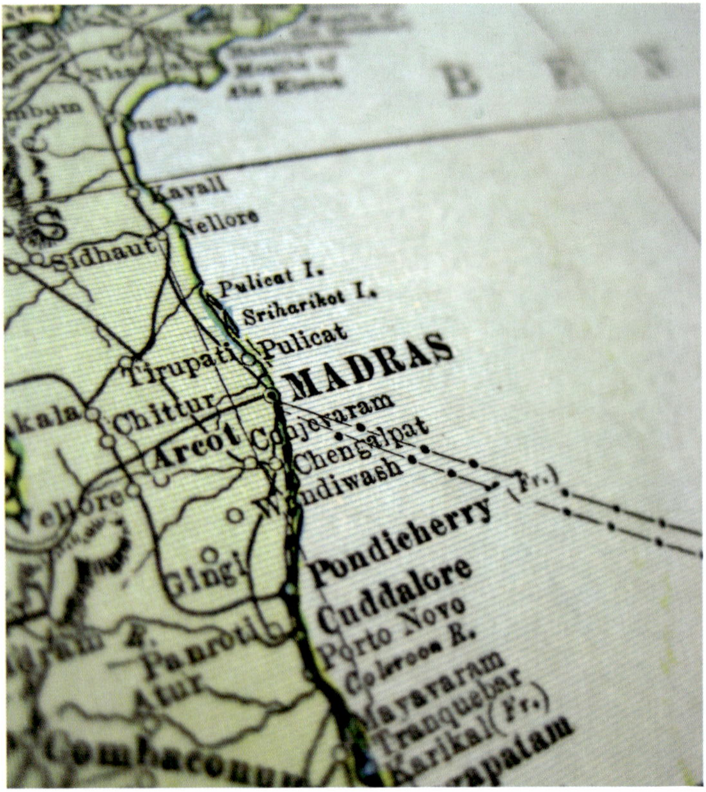

PART TWO
THE PACIFIC OCEAN

CHAPTER 12

For days, the *Tsimtsum* pushed patiently through the waves. I loved being on a ship and I followed our journey on a map. We stopped in Manila for fresh food for the animals, and the crew did some work on the ship's engines. I helped Father take care of the animals. Ravi was always in the engine room, watching the men at work. But when Ravi said there was something wrong with the engines, I didn't pay any attention.

We left Manila and entered the Pacific Ocean. On our fourth day out of Manila, we sank.

Something had woken me in the middle of the night. I think it was a loud noise. Ravi was asleep.

'Ravi!' I said. 'There was a funny noise. Let's go exploring!'

He shook his head sleepily and turned over. Oh, Ravi! I stopped outside Father and Mother's door. But Father liked his sleep so I didn't knock.

When I opened the door to the main deck, I saw the storm but I wasn't frightened. I was excited. Although I felt very brave, I also felt safe on this great ship. But then I looked up at the lifeboat. The little boat wasn't hanging straight down. Something was wrong. I ran back to the door and opened it. Inside I saw water. Lots of water. Why was there water inside? My family was down there.

Where were the officers and the crew? I saw some of

the animals, running wildly. How did they get out of their cages? There was a loud crash of metal on metal. It came from the ship. Everything was screaming: the sea, the wind, the animals, my heart. I fell over. I pulled myself up and looked over the side. I could almost touch the water. We were sinking fast.

I ran to the top deck to look for the officers. I saw three crewmen. They were pointing at something below the ship. I shouted and they saw me. They came quickly towards me.

'I'm afraid,' I shouted. 'I can't get down to my family.'

I was very grateful when they gave me a lifebelt and took hold of me in their strong arms. But then they threw me over the side of the ship.

CHAPTER 13

I landed on the tarpaulin which half-covered the lifeboat, twelve metres below. The lifeboat was hanging by ropes from the ship. It was moving wildly from side to side above the sea. I looked up at the crewmen. They were pointing at the lifeboat and shouting. What did they mean?

The crewmen didn't follow me as I expected. Instead an animal suddenly appeared in the air between them. It was a zebra. It jumped from the ship and fell with a loud crash into the lifeboat. I saw the zebra's yellow teeth as it put its head back and made a terrible noise. The ropes broke with the sudden weight of the animal. The small boat hit the water, moving quickly away from the ship on the waves.

CHAPTER 14

From the lifeboat, I saw something in the water.

'Richard Parker!' I cried. 'Is that you?' He was trying to keep his head above the water. 'Come on, Richard Parker!' I shouted. 'Swim!'

He saw me and started swimming towards the lifeboat. He looked small and afraid. His nose kept disappearing under the wild water.

'Mother! Father! Ravi! Where are you?' I shouted. 'Tell me this is a dream. Tell me I'm still in my bed on the *Tsimtsum*.'

I had no injuries on my body, but I had never known such terrible pain.

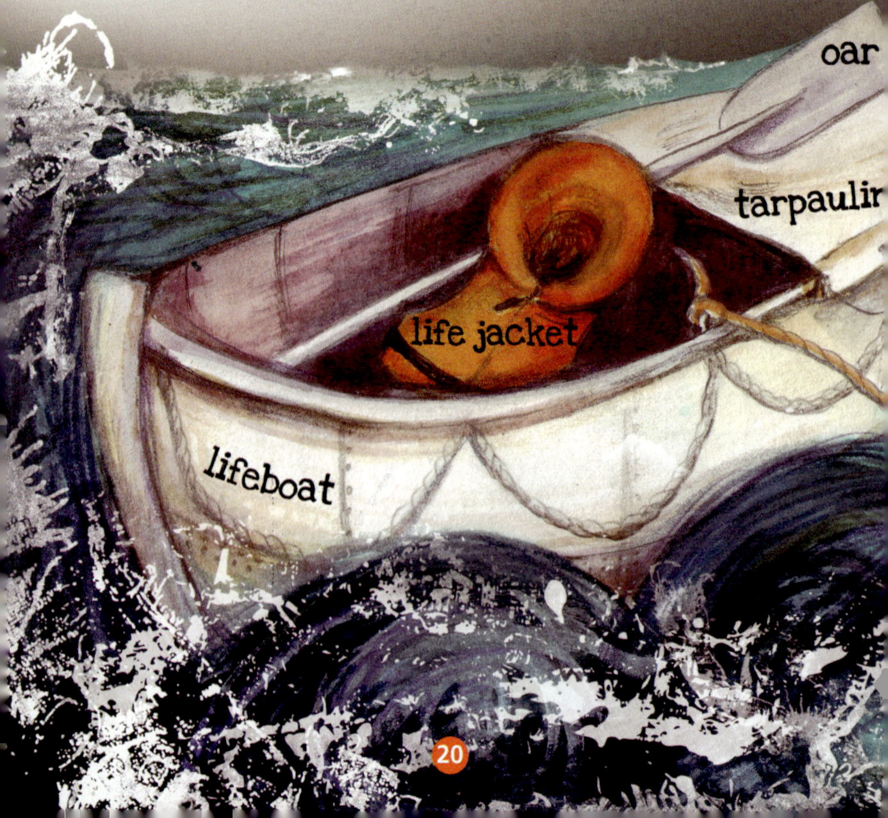

Richard Parker was moving very slowly now. I threw him a lifebelt and he took hold of it.

'Hurrah! Hold on! I'll pull you in. In a few seconds you'll be on the boat,' I shouted. Then I stopped. 'Wait a second! On the boat? Am I mad? Why am I pulling an adult Bengal tiger onto my lifeboat?'

I tried to push him away with an oar. 'Let go, Richard Parker!' I cried. But he just pulled himself onto the boat.

'Oh my God!'

Richard Parker stood up on the tarpaulin. The lifebelt fell at my feet. His fiery eyes shone angrily at me, his ears went back. His head was the same size as the lifebelt, but with teeth. I picked up the lifebelt, stepped over the zebra and threw myself into the sea.

CHAPTER 15

The water was black and cold and angry. Waves crashed down on me. And then I saw sharks. I swam as fast as I could to one end of the lifeboat, the end with the tarpaulin. The tarpaulin was tied with a strong rope to the sides of the boat. I pushed an oar into the space between the tarpaulin and the side of the boat so that the oar pointed up into the air. Then I pulled myself up and crossed my legs around the oar.

I was in the middle of the stormy ocean. I was hanging onto an oar, with an adult tiger a few metres away from me. Sharks were swimming below me. But I didn't let go of the oar. I just held on. I couldn't tell you why.

CHAPTER 16

The ship disappeared. Its lights went out. I looked for my family, for another lifeboat, for hope. There was nothing.

I was cold. My body ached. I had to move. It was still dark as I worked my way along the oar towards the boat.

'Richard Parker must be under the tarpaulin,' I thought. 'He won't smell me because I'm wet. He won't hear me because the sea is so loud.'

Carefully, I climbed up onto the tarpaulin.

Now I could see the zebra, and it was still alive. One of its back legs was broken but it was lying quietly. Why hadn't Richard Parker killed it?

Suddenly, a head appeared from under the tarpaulin. It was a hyena! So Richard Parker had not killed the zebra.

But he had also not killed the hyena. There was only one possible reason. Richard Parker was not on the boat. He had fallen off and was lost at sea.

How did the hyena get there? It was already in the lifeboat, I realised, when the crewmen threw me onto it. They knew the hyena was there. They weren't trying to save my life! They wanted me to fight the hyena. Then the boat would be safe for them. So the hyena had saved my life. And a hyena was better than a tiger in a small boat.

But a hyena was still dangerous. Hyenas look like ugly dogs with thick necks, horrible little eyes and joke ears. But they are clever fighting animals. I climbed back out onto the oar.

The sky began to change colour and soon it was the beginning of a beautiful day in the Pacific Ocean. The night had disappeared as quickly as the ship.

CHAPTER 17

She floated by on an island of bananas. The sun was behind her. Her orange hair was fiery.

'Come and join us!' I cried. It was Orange Juice, our favourite orang-utan, mother of two beautiful boys. As she stepped onto the boat, the bananas floated away. How many did I collect? None. Not a single one. I often thought of this stupid mistake in the days afterwards.

Orange Juice lay quietly on the tarpaulin for several minutes. Then she moved into the bottom of the boat. The hyena screamed. But strangely they did not fight.

CHAPTER 18

'Someone will rescue us soon!' I shouted to Orange Juice. 'We'll see a ship. They'll have a gun and shoot the hyena and the poor zebra. Just a few more hours!'

I watched for a boat all day. But I saw only sea and sky.

Later, the hyena went crazy. It ran around the zebra in circles, going 'yip yip yip' in a high voice. Finally, it stopped running. It lay down behind the zebra, coughing and being sick. It did not move for the rest of the day.

But during the night, horrible noises came from the zebra's end of the lifeboat. A fight for life was taking place and I shook with fear.

CHAPTER 19

When the sun came up, I was still alive. I thought the worst was over. 'Ravi will laugh at me,' I thought. 'He will say, "Do you think you are Noah in his Ark?" Father will look older and he will need a shave. Mother will take me in her arms.'

I looked to see what was happening in the lifeboat. The hyena had bitten off the zebra's broken leg and was eating it. The zebra was still alive and was suffering quietly.

I hated the hyena. But I did nothing. I must be honest – I couldn't worry about the zebra. I was too worried about me. I am not proud of myself, and I remember that poor zebra in my prayers every day.

It became windy in the afternoon. The boat rose and fell with every wave. Now I started to feel a little seasick.

Orange Juice was seasick too. She was lying with her mouth open and her tongue hanging out.

Hyenas and orang-utans do not meet in the wild. If they did, surely a hyena would eat an orang-utan. But nature is full of surprises. Perhaps like the goats and the rhinos, they could live together.

CHAPTER 20

Orange Juice sat up and looked across the ocean. She was looking for her family, just like me. It broke my heart.

As the sun began to set, sharks began to circle the boat. The hyena started to bite pieces off the zebra. The bottom of the boat filled with blood. The zebra suddenly coughed blood over the side of the boat. Seconds later, I heard a loud knock. Then another. The sharks had tasted the blood, and they wanted more.

Darkness came, the sharks gave up and the hyena hid behind the zebra. Silence fell. My hope disappeared with the sun. I knew my family was dead. A brother is someone you love all your life. A father teaches you how to live. A mother, well, a mother is the sun above you. I lay down on the tarpaulin and cried all night.

CHAPTER 21

The zebra died the next morning. Hyenas usually sleep in the day, especially after eating, but this hyena was watching. Orange Juice was looking dangerous.

I stayed where I was, right at the edge of the tarpaulin. I wasn't strong enough to hold onto the oar. The hyena started yipping. Suddenly, it jumped at Orange Juice. She hit it hard on the head.

'Hurrah for Orange Juice!' I shouted. An orang-utan is strong with long arms and big teeth, but it is a fruit eater. It knows nothing about fighting.

The hyena killed Orange Juice.

I was next. That much was clear to me. I had to kill the hyena or it would kill me. I walked across the tarpaulin and stepped down onto a bench. I was ready to fight the hyena. Its mouth was red with blood. Orange Juice lay next to it, against the dead zebra.

I was about to hit the hyena, when I looked down. Between my feet, under the bench, I saw Richard Parker's head. It was huge. I saw his paws. They were huge. I hurried back to the edge of the tarpaulin.

I was on a lifeboat with a tiger.

CHAPTER 22

Richard Parker got his name by mistake. A man called Richard Parker found a young tiger drinking from a river in a forest in Bangladesh. Mr Parker called it Thirsty and sold it to the Pondicherry Zoo. At the railway station in Bangladesh, an official filled in the papers for sending a tiger on the train. He wasn't paying attention. In the box marked 'Sender', he wrote Thirsty. In the box marked 'Animal's name', he wrote Richard Parker. Father laughed when he saw the papers. The tiger had a new name.

CHAPTER 23

In the morning I felt so tired. For two and a half days, I had had no food, water or sleep. And I had not noticed a 200-kilo Bengal tiger in an eight-metre-long lifeboat.

Did I lose all hope at that point? Yes. And as a result, I felt much better. I had a chance against a hyena. I had no chance against a tiger. So I stopped worrying. Now I was thirsty.

As soon as I realised I was thirsty, I could think of nothing else. I had to have water. A light went on in my head – I was on a ship's lifeboat. There had to be drinking water somewhere on the boat. All I had to do was find it.

I started to look for the water. The hyena was hiding behind the zebra. I was in no danger. It would not touch the tiger's food. I was the tiger's food.

CHAPTER 24

It said in big black letters on the side of the lifeboat that it was one metre deep, two-point-five metres wide and eight metres long. It could hold thirty people. There were narrow benches along both sides, and wider benches at each end. There were three benches across the centre, with space underneath. One of these was hidden under the tarpaulin, in Richard Parker's space.

CHAPTER 25

Where was the drinking water? I had looked everywhere except under the tarpaulin. My need for water pushed me on. Rope held the tarpaulin to the edge of the boat all the way round. Carefully, I undid the rope in two places. I looked into Richard Parker's space.

I saw several orange life jackets. I saw the orange back of a tiger. He was lying flat on his stomach. He was not moving. Perhaps he was sleeping. Perhaps he was seasick.

There was a cupboard under the seat of the bench. 'God help me!' I thought. I had to have water. I reached down and opened the door. Christmas, birthday and Diwali came all at the same time! There were golden cans with the words 'Drinking Water 500ml' on the side of each one. The first can felt cool and heavy in my shaking hand. I opened it. I opened my mouth. I poured in the water.

'Ahh!' I said, throwing the can over my shoulder and immediately getting another one. I drank two litres of wonderful water. I had never felt better in my life.

Next: food. I found half-kilo packets of ship's biscuits, made in Norway. A ship's biscuit is a thick, heavy biscuit. I bit into one. Lord, what a wonderful taste! 'Do not eat more than six biscuits in any twenty-four hours,' it said. I ate nine in half an hour.

There were instructions, explaining how much food and water one person needed each day. There was enough food for 93 days and enough water for 124 days! I spent a happy afternoon lifting one wonderful object after another out of the cupboard. There was a notebook and two ballpoint pens. I kept a list of everything that I found.

List of items found in bench cupboard:

192 seasickness pills
124 cans of fresh water – 62 litres total
31 packets of ship's biscuits, eac
packet containing 18 biscuits
16 blankets
12 solar stills
10 orange life jackets + 10 whistle
6 flares
5 oars
3 thick plastic bags (extra large)
2 boxes of matches
2 pens
2 orange buckets

2 x 50-metre orange plastic ropes
2 fishing kits
1 large knife
1 mirror
1 large bar of dark chocolate
1 book: How to Survive at Sea
1 notebook with 98 pages
1 boy with clothes but only one shoe
1 hyena
1 Bengal tiger
1 lifeboat
1 ocean
1 God

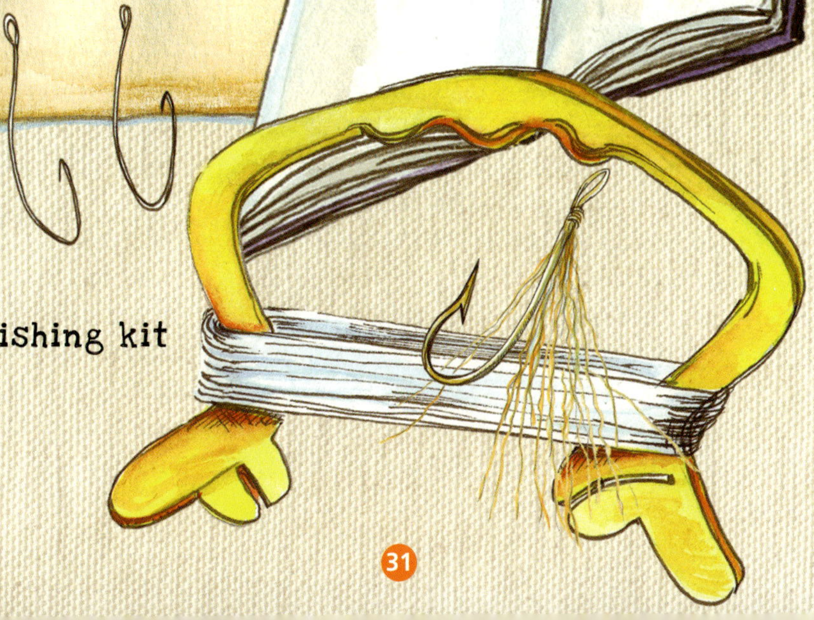
fishing kit

I climbed onto the oar and fell asleep. I slept all morning. After the water, food and sleep, I felt strong enough to see my problem clearly. There was a tiger in my lifeboat.

I could not swim away. I was hundreds of kilometres from land. I could not stay on the lifeboat. Tigers move silently. I would not hear him coming. He would kill me.

I nearly gave up then, but I heard a voice in my heart. 'I will not die,' it said. 'I will survive this nightmare. God is with me.'

Richard Parker started to growl at that moment.

'Quick, man, quick!' I said to myself. I built a raft out of the lifebelt, the oars and the life jackets. I tied them all together with the ropes.

The hyena began to scream, but then it suddenly fell silent. I looked up.

'Jesus, Muhammad and Vishnu!'

Richard Parker was standing on a bench in the middle of the boat, five metres from me. The size of him!

He killed the hyena without a sound. Then he let go of the dead animal and looked out to sea. Richard Parker's tongue was hanging from his mouth. He stood with his feet wide apart and shook his head. The movement of the boat was upsetting him. He slowly turned his head, until he was looking straight at me. He was beautiful and strong, like a king. He raised one of his lips and I saw a tooth. It was as long as my longest finger. Every hair on my body was standing up.

That's when the rat appeared. Richard Parker looked as surprised as I was. It jumped onto the tarpaulin and ran up my body and onto the top of my head. I felt its little feet holding on tight.

Richard Parker turned and dropped to the floor of the

boat. His ears were back against his head. He was ready to attack. But he seemed uncertain about the tarpaulin. For a second, he looked away.

I took hold of the rat and threw it. It sailed through the air and into Richard Parker's open mouth. The tiger seemed happy for now. He turned away and started to eat the rat. This was my chance.

I used the long rope to tie the raft to the lifeboat. My fingers were shaking. I pushed the raft off the lifeboat. If it did not float, I was dead.

It floated beautifully. I pulled the raft towards the lifeboat and jumped onto it. I waited for the raft to turn over and drop me into the sea. I waited for a shark to bite through the raft and then me. Neither happened. Sharks came close, but they did not attack.

The raft floated about thirteen metres behind the lifeboat. It felt dangerously small for the Pacific Ocean. I didn't feel safe. I took hold of the rope and pulled myself back to the boat. Then I heard Richard Parker. He was eating the hyena. I let the raft float away from the boat again. I had to choose between a tiger and sharks. I chose sharks.

CHAPTER 27

My first night on the raft was horrible. It rained and I shook with cold. I kept checking the ropes in the darkness. During the long, cold hours, I made plans to save my life.

Plan 1: Push him off the lifeboat.

Bad idea – tigers are good swimmers.

Plan 2: Attack him.

Use the flares, oars and knife. No chance!

Plan 3: Wait for him to die.

I had food and water. He didn't. Good. No animal can live without water. I had a plan and it was a good one.

CHAPTER 28

The next morning, the sky cleared and the sea was like a mirror. The sun warmed me and I fell asleep.

When I awoke, the first thing I saw was a large Bengal tiger. I heard a voice in my head. 'Plan 3 is a bad plan. When Richard Parker goes crazy because he is hungry and thirsty, he will simply swim to the raft and eat you. You will die!'

CHAPTER 29

For the moment, Richard Parker had eaten hyena and drunk rainwater, and he was happy. He looked like a nice, fat house cat. He made a strange noise through his nose. My father had told me about this noise, although I had never heard it before. It meant Richard Parker was feeling friendly towards me.

I realised that I had to be the boss. It was not a question of him or me, it was him and me. We would live – or die – together.

I had the perfect place to train him – there was nowhere for him to hide. The sea was full of fish to give him when he did well. I had whistles to show him I was boss.

I stood up on the raft. 'Ladies and gentlemen! Please hurry to your seats!' I shouted. 'The show is about to begin. It's the Greatest Show on Earth! The Pi Patel Floating Pacific Show with real live tiger!'

I blew the whistle. At the sound of the whistle, Richard Parker roared. He lifted his big paw into the air. But he did not jump into the sea to attack me. Instead he dropped to the bottom of the boat. He was afraid. My first training lesson was a big success and I had a new plan.

Plan 4: Keep him alive.

CHAPTER 30

I pulled out the book *How to Survive at Sea*. It was full of information, such as:

- Always read instructions carefully.
- Do not drink seawater or bird blood.
- If you press the eyes of a fish, the fish will not be able to move.
- Play games to keep your mind busy.
- Green water is shallower than blue water.
- Do not go swimming. The lifeboat may move faster than you can swim.
- Keep out of the sun.
- Sing and tell stories.
- Good luck!

There was also a lot of information about sailing. I studied everything. One important subject was missing: what to do with a tiger in your lifeboat.

CHAPTER 31

I made a list.

1. Teach Richard Parker that his territory is the floor of the boat as far as the middle bench. My territory is the top of the tarpaulin and the other end of the boat.

2. Start fishing.

3. Make a tent on the raft to keep the sun off me.

4. Tie a second rope between the raft and the boat in case the first one breaks.

5. Find a way to stay dry on the raft.

6. Stop expecting a ship to rescue me.

I started to cry. My future was hopeless.

CHAPTER 32

Water was a worry. The cans would not last forever. A solar still, I discovered, uses the sun's heat to produce drinking water from seawater. I tied the twelve stills together and dropped them into the sea, but I didn't expect anything to happen.

I made a tent for the raft with one of the oars, some rope and a blanket. It took me all day. I sat on the raft, had a supper of biscuits and water, and watched the sun go down.

Richard Parker sat up. I could see his head and shoulders. 'Hello, Richard Parker!' I shouted and waved to him. He looked at me and made that strange happy tiger sound again.

I looked down at the sea and discovered what looked like a city. Fish of all colours moved like buses, cars, bicycles and people on foot. It was like Tokyo at six o'clock in the evening.

For the first time, I felt a little bit of hope. I said a Muslim prayer and fell asleep.

CHAPTER 33

I had to learn to fish. I had a fishing line. What could I put on the end of it? I pulled myself to the lifeboat and searched the cupboard for ideas. Richard Parker was sitting at the end of the boat, looking back at me. Then suddenly, something hit me hard across the face. I cried out and closed my eyes, waiting for Richard Parker to hit me again and kill me. Nothing happened. I opened one eye.

It was a fish. A fish had hit me in the face. It had wings. A flying fish! And then there were fish everywhere. A whole school of them flew across, some landing in the boat. Bigger fish were chasing the flying fish into the air. Sharks were chasing the bigger fish.

Richard Parker had no difficulty catching them. Some flew into his open mouth. Others he hit with his huge paws. After a few minutes, the sea was quiet again. But the boat was full of fish. I put a blanket around one and took it to the raft.

After a lifetime as a vegetarian, it was hard for me to kill a fish. Tears were running down my face. Now I was a killer. I always include that first fish in my prayers.

The next day, I cut it into pieces and tried fishing with it. After many hours, I had my first success. With great difficulty, I pulled a big, fat fish onto the raft. This time, killing it was no problem. I hit it on the head until it stopped moving. After crying over a little fish, I happily murdered a much bigger one. I was amazed at the things I did.

I pulled the raft up to the lifeboat, threw the big fish into the boat and blew my whistle loudly. 'There you are, Richard Parker. Your fresh food comes from me, and don't forget it!'

CHAPTER 34

I looked at the clear sky and worried about water. There were enough cans of water for me, but not for a Bengal tiger. There could be many days with no rain. I checked the solar stills. Each one had a thick plastic bag under it. I put my hand in the water to feel one. It was full of fresh water! I pulled it out. One whole litre, collected in two days. I drank a litre without stopping. I emptied the other eleven bags into a bucket and took it across to Richard Parker. I carefully placed it on the side bench. His face disappeared into it and he drank. When he looked up, I looked straight into his eyes and blew the whistle. In this way, with water, fish and a whistle, I trained a huge tiger.

CHAPTER 35

I survived 227 days.

I had no idea where I was going. The wind and the sea decided where I went. I found out later that I had travelled towards the east.

I became wild. I killed fish in any way I could – with my hands, with my knife. I began to eat every part of the fish I caught, including the eyes. I could put any horrible thing in my mouth, but not if it tasted of salt. I hated salt. I still hate it today.

I allowed myself two biscuits every eight hours. I thought about food all the time.

I had only one book – *How to Survive at Sea*. I read it at least ten thousand times.

I kept a diary.

I hardly ever smiled.

I sang 'Happy Birthday' out loud to Mother on her birthday. At least, I think it was her birthday.

Life on a lifeboat isn't much of a life.

CHAPTER 36

It's hard to believe that I survived. Three things stopped Richard Parker from killing me. He was not a good sailor. He believed that I was the top cat. And he knew that I brought him food and fresh water. I began to spend more time on the tarpaulin. It was more comfortable and I did not get so wet. Richard Parker did not attack me, even when I was asleep. In the fight for number one position, I had won.

CHAPTER 37

The storm built up slowly. I brought in the solar stills. Mountains and valleys formed in the sea. As the storm became worse, I pulled the tarpaulin across the whole of the boat. I tied it tightly down over us both. Richard Parker was somewhere on the floor of the boat. I held onto the narrow bench where the cupboard was. For a day and a night, we rose and fell on the waves. Each time we came down, the boat filled with water.

When the storm was over, I undid the tarpaulin and lay on top of it. Two oars and a life jacket floated behind the boat. My raft had gone. Thank God – the water bags in the cupboard were still there. But the sea had washed most of our food away.

CHAPTER 38

'Richard Parker! A ship!' I shouted. 'We're saved!'

It was coming right towards us. 'Thank you, Allah, Lord of all Worlds!' I stood up for the first time in a long time. My legs were very weak now.

The ship came closer. 'Can you believe it, Richard Parker? People, food, a bed!'

The ship came closer still. It looked like a ship carrying oil. It had steep black sides with no windows.

Hope filled my heart. I thought about my family. There were many lifeboats on the *Tsimtsum*. Perhaps my family had reached Canada weeks ago and were waiting for news of me.

The ship was like a mountain moving slowly towards us. It was very close. 'It needs to turn soon,' I said. And then I realised. Richard Parker realised and he roared. A huge wave circled the ship where it pushed through the water. 'It's going to run us over!'

The wave pushed us up in the air. The ship missed us by less than a metre.

It took minutes to pass us. I fired a flare. It hit the side of the ship and fell back into the sea. I shouted as loudly as I could. I blew my whistle.

The ship disappeared. We looked at each other. Richard Parker knew something bad had happened. He saw the pain in my eyes. He lay down and went to sleep.

'I love you!' I said to him. 'I couldn't survive without you. I'll get you to land, I promise!'

CHAPTER 39

The sun and the saltwater were slowly destroying everything, including us. Richard Parker's fur began to fall off. The sun burnt off my clothes. We were both very thin. We slept most of the time.

I wrote in my diary:

I feel terrible.

R.P. is alive but not moving. We will die soon. He will not kill me.

ONE HOUR LATER

We've just had some beautiful rain! I've filled the water bags and my body.

R.P. still isn't moving. I touched him for the first time. His body felt warm. He lifted his head and drank. Then he ate some fish. He's gone back to sleep now.

It's no use. Today we will die.

The diary ends there. The pens ran out.

CHAPTER 40

Richard Parker began to rub his eyes with his paw. He made unhappy noises. When I caught a fish, I threw half to him. Usually he caught it in his open mouth, but this time it hit him in the face.

'Richard Parker, have you gone blind?' I said. I waved my hand in front of his nose.

The next day, my eyes felt uncomfortable. I rubbed them and they got worse. Then darkness came. I could not take care of Richard Parker if I could not see. I closed my eyes and waited to die.

I heard the words, 'Is someone there?'

You hear strange things when you're alone in the darkness.

The words came again. 'Is someone there?'

'Yes, I'm here,' I said. Had I gone mad?

The voice came back again. 'Let's talk about food ...'

'What a good idea,' I said.

'Describe your perfect meal,' said the voice. I described all my favourite dishes – India's best vegetarian dishes! He then described his favourite dishes, which were all meat. I felt sick.

'Have you ever killed a man?' I asked.

'Yes,' said the voice. 'Two. A man and a woman.'

'Why did you kill them?' I asked.

'I had to,' he said. 'It was them or me.'

'Excuse me?' I said after a while.

'Yes?'

'Are you French? You speak English, but you sound French.'

'Please,' said the voice suddenly. It sounded closer. 'Do you have any food? I haven't eaten for days.'

'I have no food,' I said. 'Where are you?'

'I'm here,' he said.

'Where's "here"? I can't see you. I've gone blind.'

'What?' he cried. 'I too am blind.'

I had met another blind man on a lifeboat in the Pacific Ocean.

'Why are you blind?' I asked.

'Same as you,' he said. 'No food or water for months in the burning sun.'

We both started to cry. 'Come onto my boat!' I said. 'Let's be together.'

I found the oars. We moved our boats close with difficulty. He threw me a rope and I tied his boat to mine. I opened my arms to him. He jumped on top of me and we fell back onto the tarpaulin. He put his hands around my throat.

'Stop!' I tried to say. 'There's something I must tell you!'

'There's something I must tell *you*,' he said. 'I'm going to eat you!'

I pushed him off me onto the tarpaulin. He fell onto the floor of the boat.

'No!' I shouted.

Too late! The voice screamed loudly. I smelt blood. Richard Parker was eating him.

Crying was good for my eyes. Two days later, I could see again. Eating was good for Richard Parker. His sight returned too.

CHAPTER 41

One afternoon, I saw trees with bright green leaves. Were my eyes playing tricks on me? The trees grew into a forest. It was an island!

We came close. The island seemed to be made of some kind of strange seaweed.

'Richard Parker! Land! We're saved!' I shouted.

My legs were weak but I pulled myself onto the island. I cut bits off the thick seaweed. It smelt fresh and I tried eating it. The outside was salty. But the inside tasted wonderful. It was as sweet as sugar! I ate and ate.

I heard a noise and turned. Richard Parker jumped from the boat. Like me, he found it hard to stand. He moved across the island slowly, and disappeared into the trees.

In the late afternoon, with a stomach full of sweet seaweed, I returned to the boat. I lay on the tarpaulin – my territory. I was afraid Richard Parker would attack me if he met me on land. I fell asleep. A noise in the night woke me. Richard Parker had come back to the boat too, and he was in pain. He was rubbing his paws against his nose.

'Richard Parker, are your paws hurting?' I asked. He was soon quiet and I fell asleep again.

After a wonderful night's sleep, I ate more seaweed for breakfast. Richard Parker waited for hours before jumping off the boat. He lifted his paws angrily in the air, but then he disappeared as on the first day.

The next few days were the same. We both became stronger. I learnt to walk again. Richard Parker became a wild animal who could run at high speed. We spent our days on the island and our nights on the boat. I still seemed to be the boss on the boat. The whistle still worked.

I decided to explore the island. I walked up to a high point and looked down the other side. The whole island was made of seaweed, with a green forest at its centre. There were small pools of water all around the forest.

And for the first time, I saw the meerkats! Yes, meerkats! Hundreds and thousands of them. This side of the island was covered in them. When I appeared, they all stood up and looked at me. They showed no fear and quickly lost interest. They went back to eating the seaweed or looking into the pools.

I came to one of the pools. What were the meerkats looking at? Suddenly, the pool filled with fish. The meerkats went crazy. Some threw themselves into the water after the fish. But the fish were dead and the meerkats simply had to pull them out.

I put my hand in the water. It was cool. I could feel colder water coming up from below with the fish. I tasted it. It was fresh water! So these sea fish had died because they could not live in fresh water. Perhaps the seaweed took the salt out of the seawater. I laughed out loud and jumped into the pool. The fresh water felt wonderful on my poor skin.

Later, I saw Richard Parker some way off. He was moving through the meerkats, eating one after another, blood all over his face. The meerkats had no idea of danger.

Slowly, Richard Parker and I returned to life. I ate, drank and bathed. I watched the meerkats. I walked and ran and rested. My skin looked healthy again. My aches and pains disappeared. Richard Parker became fatter, his fur became thicker and his eyes began to shine again.

Nothing lived on the island except seaweed, trees, meerkats, one tiger and one boy. In fact, the trees seemed to be joined to the seaweed. The island was floating, and it wasn't an island at all.

It was crazy to sleep each night on the boat, one metre above a Bengal tiger. There was a whole island out there! I decided to sleep in a tree. Although Richard Parker never seemed to leave the boat at night, he might suddenly decide to go for a midnight walk. If he found me outside my territory, I would be in trouble. I climbed up with some blankets just as it was getting dark.

I discovered that the meerkats all slept in the trees too. They climbed noisily up to me, over me and about me. They all lay down and we fell asleep. As soon as the sun came up, they returned noisily to the ground.

One night, the meerkats woke me up. The pool below the tree was filled with fish. Dead fish. The meerkats screamed excitedly, but not a single one went down to the pool. The next morning, the pool was empty. Where were the fish?

The answer to this mystery came later when I was deep in the forest. I noticed a tree with strange fruit. None of the other trees had fruit. I picked one. The fruit was not a fruit. It was a ball of leaves. Inside I found a human tooth. Each fruit contained a tooth. There were thirty-two teeth. Humans have thirty-two teeth. I felt sick and angry.

That night, I climbed into my usual tree but I did not sleep. I picked up a meerkat and dropped it onto the ground. It ran screaming back to the tree. I climbed down myself. I gently put my feet on the ground. A terrible pain ran up through my feet. I screamed. I managed to pull myself back into the tree. My feet burnt all night.

The island was a meat-eater. It ate the saltwater fish in the pools. It ate any meerkat that was on the ground after dark. It had slowly killed and eaten the owner of the teeth.

That's why Richard Parker slept in the boat. That's why nothing else lived on the island.

The next morning, I filled the big plastic bags with fresh water. I drank as much as I could. I collected fish from the pools and dead meerkats. I cut off a huge piece of seaweed and tied it behind the boat.

I waited for Richard Parker. If I left him behind, he would die. He would not survive the first night. As soon as he returned and jumped onto the lifeboat, we left the island. The seaweed was gone the next day. It had eaten through the rope during the night.

CHAPTER 42

The rest of our time at sea was nothing but pain.

When we finally reached land, I was too weak to be happy. As I climbed over the side of the boat, Richard Parker jumped over me and onto the beach. He didn't look at me. He ran along the sand to the edge of the rainforest. Then he stopped. I waited for him to look back at me, to put his ears back and growl. I waited for him to say goodbye in some way. He did nothing of the sort. He went into the rainforest and disappeared from my life forever.

After a few hours, some people found me. They pulled the lifeboat onto the sand and carried me away. I cried like a child because Richard Parker had not said goodbye. I wanted to thank him for saving my life. I wanted to tell him to be careful of humans. I wanted to tell him that I loved him.

PART THREE

HOSPITAL, TOMATLÁN, MEXICO

CHAPTER 43

WRITER'S NOTE: *What follows is a conversation that took place in Tomatlán Hospital. Mr Okamoto and Mr Chiba came to interview Pi Patel about the sinking of the Japanese ship* Tsimtsum. *Pi was in bed. Mr Okamoto recorded the conversation. (The words in* **bold** *were spoken in Japanese. I give them here in English.)*

Today is February the 19th, 1978. In the room are myself, Mr Okamoto, my assistant, Mr Chiba, and Mr Pi Patel, only survivor of the *Tsimtsum*. Are you comfortable, Mr Patel? Now, please tell us what happened.

CHAPTER 44

The story.

CHAPTER 45

Mr Okamoto: Very interesting.

Mr Chiba: What a story.

Mr Okamoto: **He thinks we're stupid.** Mr Patel, we'll take a little break.

Pi: That's fine. I'd like another biscuit.

Mr Chiba: **He's not eating the biscuits – he's hiding them under his bedclothes.**

Mr Okamoto: **Just give him another one.** We'll be back in a few minutes.

CHAPTER 46

Mr Okamoto: Mr Patel, we don't believe your story.

Pi: I'm amazed. Why not?

Mr Okamoto: Bananas don't float. You said the orang-utan arrived floating on an island of bananas.

Pi: Yes, they do. Here, I've got two bananas. Fill the sink with water and try these.

Mr Chiba: **What else has he got in his bed?**

Mr Okamoto: **Oh dear. This is going to be a long day.**

[Sound of water running]

Pi: Are they floating?

Mr Okamoto: Yes, they're floating.

Pi: Could I have my bananas back?

Mr Chiba: I'll get them.

Mr Okamoto: This island. Seaweed that eats fish. Trees that eat men. These things don't exist.

Pi: Only because you've never seen them.

Mr Okamoto: That's right. We believe what we see.

Pi: What do you do when you're in the dark?

Mr Okamoto: Why has nobody else seen it?

Pi: Big ships cross the ocean quickly. I went slowly, looking at everything.

Mr Okamoto: We're not sure about the tiger either. How could you survive in a lifeboat with a tiger?

Pi: Wild animals are afraid of us. They only fight when there is no other way out.

Mr Okamoto: Where is it now? If there was a tiger out there, the police would know about it.

Pi: You expect to find a tiger in a Mexican rainforest! Ha, ha, ha!

Mr Okamoto: What about this Frenchman? The one in the other lifeboat. You say he knew a lot about food. The cook on the *Tsimtsum* was a Frenchman. Maybe you met the cook.

Pi: How should I know? I never saw his face. I was blind, remember? Then Richard Parker ate him. By the way, how do you explain the meerkat bones in the lifeboat?

Mr Okamoto: Yes, the bones of small animals were found. They were probably from the ship.

Pi: We had no meerkats at the zoo.

Mr Okamoto: Well, we cannot explain these bones. We are here because a Japanese ship sank in the Pacific.

Pi: I never forget that. I lost my whole family.

Mr Okamoto: We're very sorry about that.

Pi: Not as sorry as me.

Mr Chiba: **What do we do now?**

Mr Okamoto: **I don't know.**

[Long silence]

Mr Okamoto: We would like to know what really happened.

Pi: So you want another story?

Mr Okamoto: We want the facts.

Pi: You want a story without animals.

Mr Okamoto: Yes!

Pi: Here's another story.

Mr Okamoto: Good!

CHAPTER 47

Pi: The ship sank and I found myself in the Pacific Ocean. I swam for the lifeboat. The cook threw me a lifebelt and pulled me in. Four of us survived: Mother, the cook, a sailor and me.

The sailor had broken his leg when he jumped from the ship. His suffering was terrible. His leg went bad. The cook said we must cut it off. We had nothing to take away the pain, so we did it quickly. Mother and I held the sailor's arms and the cook sat on his good leg. The sailor screamed. He cried from the pain all night. Mother gave him water.

The sailor died. The cook cut him into pieces for fishing. Mother hated him for it. The next time the cook came close, Mother hit him. She did it for the poor sailor. The cook could not look her in the eyes. We each had our end of the lifeboat. I stayed close to Mother. She saw him eat a piece of the sailor. She called him an animal.

But the cook was useful. He knew about the sea and he built the raft to fish from. Mother and I ate the fish that the cook caught. Mother had been a vegetarian all her life and she found it hard.

We managed for a while. It was exciting when the cook caught a big fish. He and Mother sometimes talked or even joked. He said our best hope was to watch for an island. And when we were busy watching for an island, he helped himself to food and water from the lifeboat.

One day, we had no food left. I was too weak to hold onto a turtle. Because of me, we lost it and the cook hit me. Mother hit him back. He caught her arm and broke it. She screamed and fell. He picked up the knife and killed her. He threw her body into the sea.

I spent a day and night on the raft. He didn't cut me loose. In the morning, I pulled myself into the lifeboat. He said nothing. He knew he had done a terrible thing and he wanted to die. He left the knife on the bench. I used it to kill him.

I was alone. I turned to God. I survived.

[Long silence]

CHAPTER 48

Pi: Is that better?

Mr Chiba: **What a horrible story!**

Mr Okamoto: **Both the zebra and the sailor broke a leg, did you notice that?**

Mr Chiba: **No, I didn't.**

Mr Okamoto: **And the hyena bit off the zebra's leg. The cook cut off the sailor's leg. The blind Frenchman in the first story – he said he'd killed a man and a woman. The cook killed the sailor and his mother.**

Mr Chiba: **Oh, Mr Okamoto, you're right!**

Mr Okamoto: **So the sailor is the zebra, his mother is the orang-utan, the cook is ... the hyena ... which means that he's the tiger!**

Mr Chiba: **But what about the island? And the meerkats? And the teeth in the tree! Whose are those?**

Mr Okamoto: **I have no idea. I'm not inside this boy's head.**

[Long silence]

Mr Okamoto: Mr Patel, do you know why the ship sank?

Pi: No. You tell me.

Mr Okamoto: Thank you, Mr Patel. I think we have all we need.

Pi: I have a question for you. In both stories the ship sinks, my family dies and I suffer. Which is the better story?

Mr Okamoto: That's an interesting question ...

Mr Chiba: The story with animals.

Pi: Thank you. And so it goes with God.

[Silence]

CHAPTER 49

Mr Okamoto: What will you do now?

Pi: I guess I'll go to Canada.

Mr Okamoto: You won't go back to India?

Pi: There's nothing there for me now.

Mr Okamoto: Of course you will receive some money from the company.

Pi: Thank you.

Mr Okamoto: **Come on, I'm hungry. You can turn that off.**

CHAPTER 50

WRITER'S NOTE

Mr Okamoto sent me a copy of his report. It was not known why the ship sank, he wrote. He ended his report: 'Mr Pi Patel was the only person to survive. He was very brave. Very few people have survived so long at sea, and none in the company of an adult Bengal tiger.'

THE END

30 PERSONS

THREE RELIGIONS

These three religions are the largest in the world with around 4.5 billion followers.

Hinduism

Hinduism is the world's oldest religion. It has existed for 4,000 years. Today, 80% of Indians are Hindus. It is also the third most popular religion in Britain.

God: There is one God, called Brahman. There are many gods and goddesses, but they are all forms of Brahman. Ganesha, for example, is the elephant god, and helps you do well in life.

Holy book: There are many Hindu holy books. These are called Veda.

Holy building: The temple

Holy place: The River Ganges in north India. Hindus bathe in the river.

Fireworks at Diwali

How they live: Hindus believe in reincarnation (being reborn). They try to live a good life so that they will be born into a better life when they die.

Main festival: Diwali – the 'festival of lights'. Hindus have lights in their homes and there are fireworks. They give presents to family and friends.

Islam

Islam is the world's second largest religion, and the second largest religion in Britain too. It has more than two billion followers, who are called Muslims.

God: There is one God, known as Allah.

Holy book: The Qur'an. It is a message from Allah, given to the prophet Muhammad.

Holy building: The mosque

Holy place: Mecca, in Saudi Arabia. All Muslims must try to travel to Mecca once in their lives. This journey is called a pilgrimage.

How they live: Muslims follow five rules, known as the Five Pillars of Islam. These include fasting and praying five times a day.

Christianity

The Christian religion is the world's largest, and the main religion in Britain. Christian countries count their years from the birth of Jesus Christ. The year 2000 was two thousand years after his birth.

God: There is only one God. Jesus Christ is the son of God.

Holy book: The Bible. It describes the life of Jesus and his death on the cross.

Holy building: The church

Holy place: Bethlehem, where Jesus was born.

How they live: Christians follow the example of Jesus Christ, who taught people to love others, even those who are unkind to them.

Singing carols at Christmas

Is there anything which is similar about these main festivals?

Main festival: Christmas (Christ's birthday). It begins on the evening before Christmas Day, when families sing special songs, called carols, and go to church. The next day there is a big family lunch, and presents for everyone.

A pilgrimage to Mecca

Main festival: Eid-ul-Fitr. This festival begins on the last day of Ramadan, after a month of fasting. Everyone says the Eid prayer, and there is a special meal.

What do these words mean? You can use a dictionary.

festival fireworks prophet cross fasting

PART ONE: CHAPTERS 1–11

Before you read

You can use your dictionary.

1 Choose the correct noun to complete these sentences.

cage cricket growls holy human priest temple

- **a)** My cousin has a rat, which she keeps in a ... .
- **b)** If you want to join a religion, you can talk to a ... .
- **c)** ... is India's national sport.
- **d)** Neil Armstrong was the first ... to walk on the moon in 1969.
- **e)** A dog ... before it attacks.
- **f)** If a thing or place is special in a religion, it is ... .
- **g)** In some religions, people pray in a ... .

2 Look at 'People and places' on pages 4–5.

- **a)** Why does Pi love animals, do you think?
- **b)** Where do Pi's family live when he is a boy?
- **c)** Where is the *Tsimtsum* sailing to? What ocean does it cross?
- **d)** How old is Pi when his amazing adventure starts?

After you read

3 Choose the best answers.

- **a)** Who is 'I' in the Writer's Note on page 6?
  Pi ☐ the writer ☐
- **b)** Who is 'I' when the story starts on page 8?
  Pi ☐ the writer ☐
- **c)** In Pi's opinion, what do animals think of life in a zoo?
  They like it. ☐ They hate it. ☐
- **d)** Which of these animals are friends in Pi's zoo?
  the rhinos and goats ☐ the tiger and the goat ☐
- **e)** Why do the Patels decide to leave Pondicherry Zoo?
  There aren't enough visitors. ☐ The work is too hard. ☐

4 What do you think?
Are zoos a good thing or a bad thing?

PART TWO: CHAPTERS 12–29

Before you read

You can use your dictionary.

5 Make sentences.

a)	A big ship has	i)	four big paws.
b)	A lifeboat has	ii)	very big engines.
c)	The crew work	iii)	without food or drink for many days.
d)	A raft	iv)	on a ship.
e)	A heavy stone	v)	floats on the sea.
f)	A person suffers	vi)	sinks in water.
g)	A tiger has	vii)	benches to sit on.

After you read

6 Answer the questions.

a) What happened to the ship four days after they left Manila?
b) What happened to Pi when the crewmen threw him over the side of the ship?
c) Why did the lifeboat break away from the ship?
d) What did Pi do when Richard Parker climbed onto the lifeboat?
e) Pi thought that Richard Parker had fallen off the lifeboat. Why?
f) Why didn't Pi help the zebra?

7 Are these sentences true or false? Correct the false sentences.

a) The orang-utan kills the hyena.
b) Before Richard Parker came to the zoo, his name was Thirsty.
c) After Pi finds the ship's biscuits, he eats six in one day.
d) Pi eats a rat.
e) Pi plans to kill Richard Parker.

8 Which of these things can Pi do after he finds the survival cupboard?

keep warm ☐ eat ☐ build a raft ☐
make a phone call ☐ write ☐ drink ☐

9 What do you think?
Could you build a raft on your own?

PART TWO: CHAPTERS 30–42

Before you read

You can use your dictionary.

10 Put the correct word in each sentence.

blind **fur** **rub** **seaweed**

a) Don't ... your eyes if they are hurting.
b) A ... person cannot see.
c) You can find ... on the beach.
d) A Bengal tiger's ... is orange and black.

After you read

11 Choose the correct word.

a) Pi writes himself a list: it makes him feel **better / worse**.
b) Richard Parker finds it **easy / hard** to catch the flying fish.
c) Pi is **happy / upset** when he kills his first fish.
d) Pi learns that blue water is **deeper / shallower** than green water.
e) Pi sings 'Happy Birthday' on **his own / his mother's** birthday.

12 Which things does Pi use to train Richard Parker?

biscuits ☐ fish ☐ flares ☐
rope ☐ water ☐ a whistle ☐

13 Are these sentences true or false? Correct the false sentences.

a) Pi loses his raft and most of his food in a storm.
b) A ship passes one kilometre from the lifeboat.
c) Pi touches Richard Parker to check that he is still alive.
d) Pi's sight returns but Richard Parker's sight does not.
e) Richard Parker eats a man from another lifeboat.
f) The seaweed on the island is too nasty to eat.
g) The only other animals on the island are meerkats.
h) Pi has to leave the island because it wants to kill him.

14 What do you think? What things does Pi do to survive? Could *you* survive on a lifeboat?

PART THREE: CHAPTERS 43–50

Before you read

15 What do you think?

a) What happens to Pi now?

b) What happens to Richard Parker?

After you read

16 Answer the questions.

a) Why is Pi hiding his biscuits under the bedclothes?

b) What else is he hiding in his bed?

c) Why doesn't Mr Okamoto believe that the island was real?

d) What is Pi's answer to this?

e) Why doesn't he believe that the tiger was real?

f) How does Pi explain what happened to the tiger?

g) Who does Mr Okamoto think the man in the second lifeboat was?

h) How does Mr Okamoto explain the meerkat bones?

i) Why does Pi say this is not true?

17 In Pi's second story, put the names in the correct spaces.

Pi   **Pi's mother**   **the cook**   **the sailor**

a) ... threw Pi a lifebelt.

b) ... cut off the sailor's leg.

c) ... died and was cut into pieces by the cook.

d) ... hit the cook.

e) ... built the raft.

f) ... dropped a big fish.

g) ... broke Pi's mother's arm.

h) ... killed the cook.

18 What do you think?

a) Which story do you prefer?

b) Which story actually happened?

NEW WORDS

What do these words mean?

bench (n) ....

blind (adj) ....

bone (n) ....

cage (n) ....

crew (n) ....

cricket (n) ....

deck (n) ....

engine (n) ....

float (v) ....

fur (n) ....

growl (v) ....

holy (adj) ....

human (n) ....

paw (n) ....

pray (v) .... / prayer (n) ....

priest (n) ....

raft (n) ....

roar (v) ....

rub (v) ....

seaweed (n) ....

sink (v) ....

suffer (v) .... / suffering (n) ....

temple (n) ....

territory (n) ....

zoo (n) ....

ANIMAL WORDS. Are these the same in your language?
elephant, goat, hyena, lion, meerkat, orang-utan, rat, rhino, shark, tiger, turtle, zebra